KEVIN McCOLLUM

BROADWAY GLOBAL VENTURES CMC MASTRO/GOODMAN JERRY &
KYODO TOKYO INC. WENDY FEDERMAN BARBARA FREITAG LAM
TIMOTHY LACZYNSKI DAN MARKLEY HARRIS/KARMAZIN JAM T

AND

JUJAMCYN THEATERS

PRESENT

BOOK BY
KAREY KIRKPATRICK AND JOHN O'FARRELL

MUSIC AND LYRICS BY
WAYNE KIRKPATRICK AND KAREY KIRKPATRICK

CONCEIVED BY KAREY KIRKPATRICK AND WAYNE KIRKPATRICK

STARRING

BRIAN d'ARCY JAMES

JOHN CARIANI

HEIDI BLICKENSTAFF BRAD OSCAR KATE REINDERS

BROOKS ASHMANSKAS PETER BARTLETT GERRY VICHI MICHAEL JAMES SCOTT

ELIZABETH EARLEY ERIC GIANCOLA LINDA GRIFFIN DAVID HIBBARD JENNY HILL STACEY TODD HOLT
COURTNEY IVENTOSCH AARON KABURICK AUSTIN LESCH BETH JOHNSON NICELY ALEKS PEVEC
ERIC SCIOTTO BRIAN SHEPARD CHELSEA MORGAN STOCK ANGIE SCHWORER
RYAN VANDENBOOM MATT WALL MARISHA WALLACE BUD WEBER

AND

CHRISTIAN BORLE

SCENIC DESIGN	COSTUME DESIGN	LIGHTING DESIGN	SOUND DESIGN
SCOTT PASK	**GREGG BARNES**	**JEFF CROITER**	**PETER HYLENSKI**
CASTING	HAIR DESIGN	MAKEUP DESIGN	TECHNICAL SUPERVISOR
TELSEY + COMPANY BETHANY KNOX, CSA	**JOSH MARQUETTE**	**MILAGROS MEDINA-CERDEIRA**	**JUNIPER STREET PRODUCTIONS, INC**
PRODUCTION STAGE MANAGER	ASSOCIATE DIRECTOR	ASSOCIATE CHOREOGRAPHER	
CHARLES UNDERHILL	**STEVE BEBOUT**	**JOHN MACINNIS**	
ASSOCIATE PRODUCER	ADVERTISING & MARKETING	PRESS REPRESENTATIVE	GENERAL MANAGEMENT
LUCAS McMAHON	**SPOTCO**	**BONEAU/BRYAN-BROWN**	**BESPOKE THEATRICALS**
MUSIC DIRECTION & VOCAL ARRANGEMENTS	MUSIC ARRANGEMENTS	ORCHESTRATIONS	MUSIC COORDINATOR
PHIL RENO	**GLEN KELLY**	**LARRY HOCHMAN**	**JOHN MILLER**

DIRECTED AND CHOREOGRAPHED BY
CASEY NICHOLAW

DEVELOPED IN ASSOCIATION WITH THE 5TH AVENUE THEATRE, SEATTLE, WA. DAVID ARMSTRONG, EXECUTIVE PRODUCER AND
ARTISTIC DIRECTOR, BERNADINE GRIFFIN, MANAGING DIRECTOR, AND BILL BERRY, PRODUCING ARTISTIC DIRECTOR.

Cover art: SpotCo

ISBN 978-1-4950-4586-8

7777 W. BLUEMOUND RD. P.O. BOX 13819 MILWAUKEE, WI 53213

In Australia Contact:
Hal Leonard Australia Pty. Ltd.
4 Lentara Court
Cheltenham, Victoria, 3192 Australia
Email: ausadmin@halleonard.com.au

For all works contained herein:
Unauthorized copying, arranging, adapting, recording, Internet posting, public performance,
or other distribution of the printed music in this publication is an infringement of copyright.
Infringers are liable under the law.

Visit Hal Leonard Online at
www.halleonard.com

3	Welcome to the Renaissance
18	God, I Hate Shakespeare
28	Right Hand Man
36	A Musical
50	The Black Death
54	I Love the Way
63	Will Power
74	Bottom's Gonna Be on Top
89	Hard to Be the Bard
103	We See the Light
115	Make an Omelette
131	To Thine Own Self (Reprise)

WELCOME TO THE RENAISSANCE

Words and Music by
WAYNE KIRKPATRICK
and KAREY KIRKPATRICK

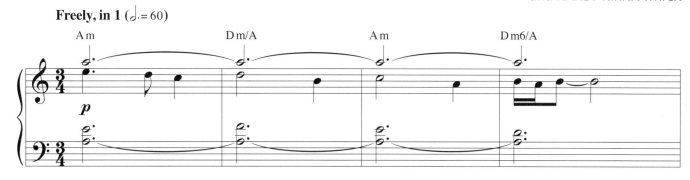

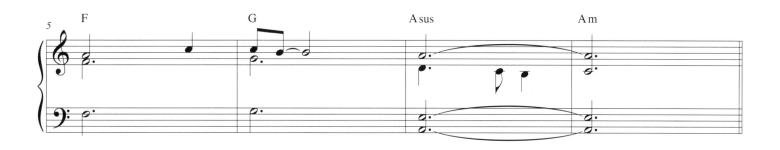

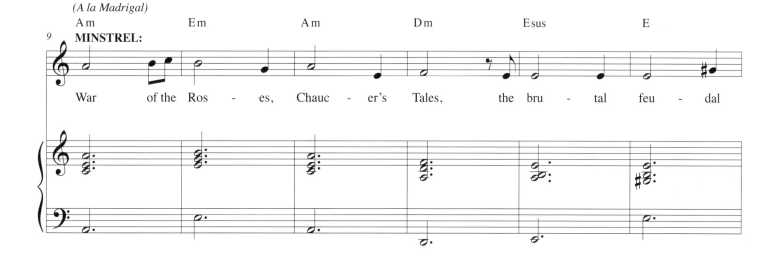

(A la Madrigal)

MINSTREL: War of the Ros - es, Chauc - er's Tales, the bru - tal feu - dal

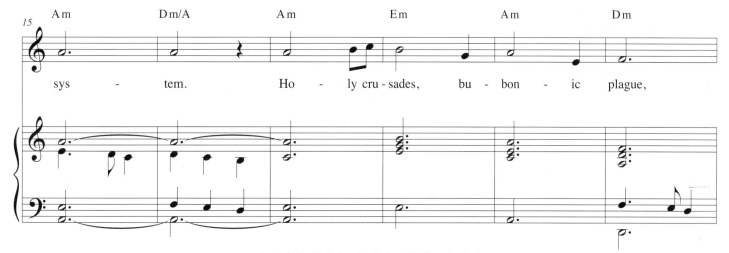

sys - tem. Ho - ly cru - sades, bu - bon - ic plague,

Copyright © 2015 Mad Mother Music and Really Rotten Music
All Rights for Mad Mother Music Administered by Razor & Tie Music Publishing, LLC
All Rights for Really Rotten Music Administered by WB Music Corp.
All Rights Reserved   Used by Permission

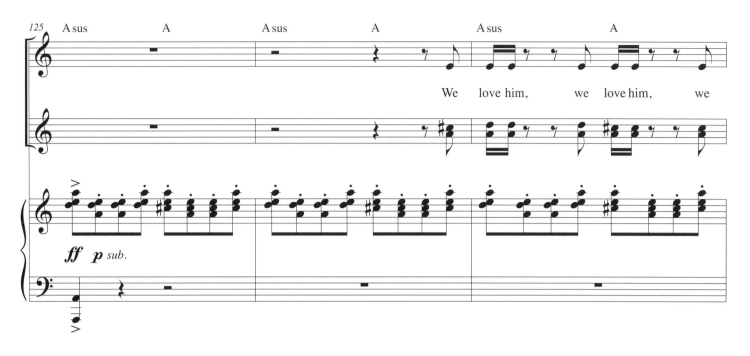

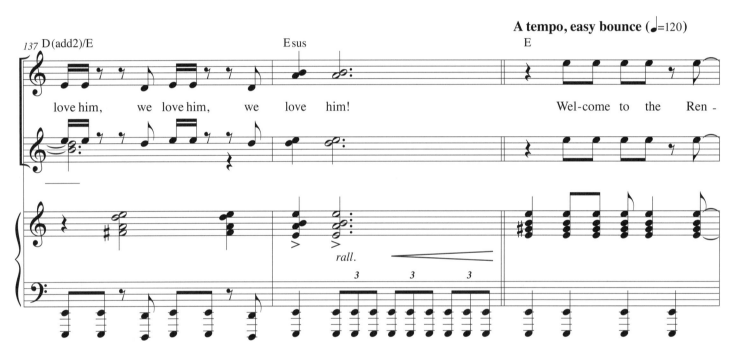

GOD, I HATE SHAKESPEARE

Words and Music by
WAYNE KIRKPATRICK
and KAREY KIRKPATRICK

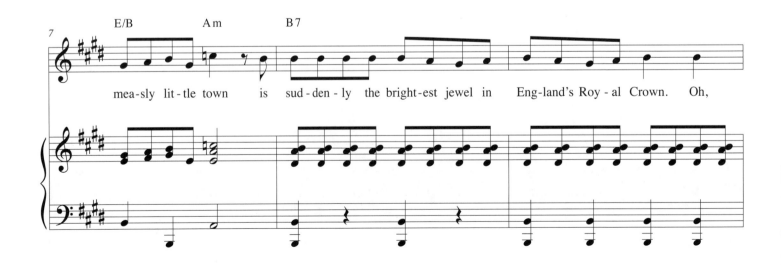

Copyright © 2015 Mad Mother Music and Really Rotten Music
All Rights for Mad Mother Music Administered by Razor & Tie Music Publishing, LLC
All Rights for Really Rotten Music Administered by WB Music Corp.
All Rights Reserved   Used by Permission

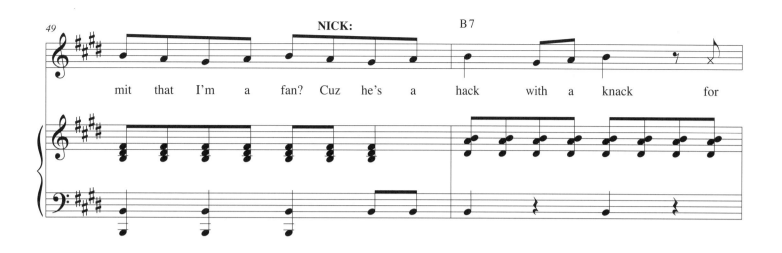

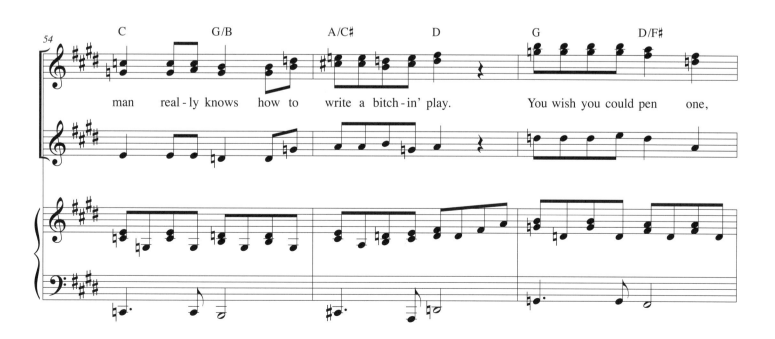

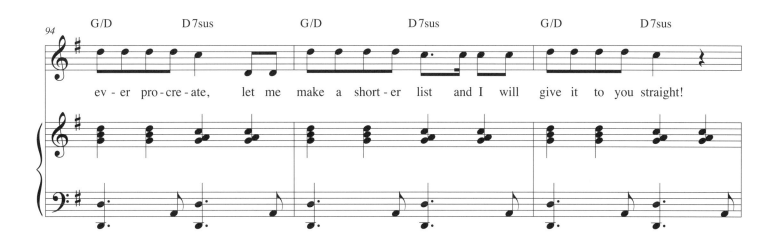

A MUSICAL

Words and Music by
WAYNE KIRKPATRICK
and KAREY KIRKPATRICK

NICK: *An actor is saying his lines and then, out of nowhere, he just starts singing??*
NOSTRADAMUS: *Yes!*

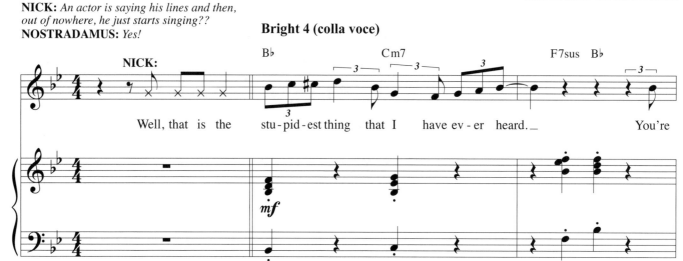

Well, that is the stu-pid-est thing that I have ev-er heard. You're

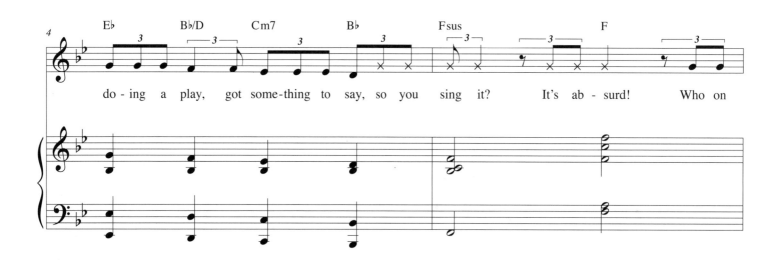

do-ing a play, got some-thing to say, so you sing it? It's ab-surd! Who on

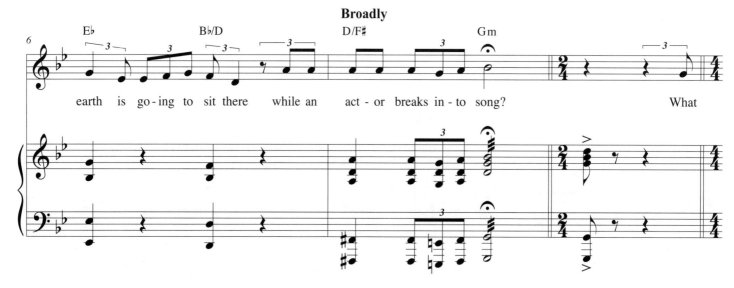

earth is go-ing to sit there while an act-or breaks in-to song? What

Copyright © 2015 Mad Mother Music and Really Rotten Music
All Rights for Mad Mother Music Administered by Razor & Tie Music Publishing, LLC
All Rights for Really Rotten Music Administered by WB Music Corp.
All Rights Reserved   Used by Permission

NICK: *I don't know, I find it hard to believe people would actually pay to see something like this.*

NOSTRADAMUS:

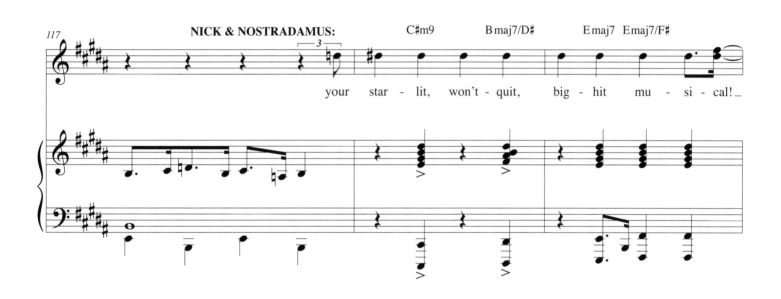
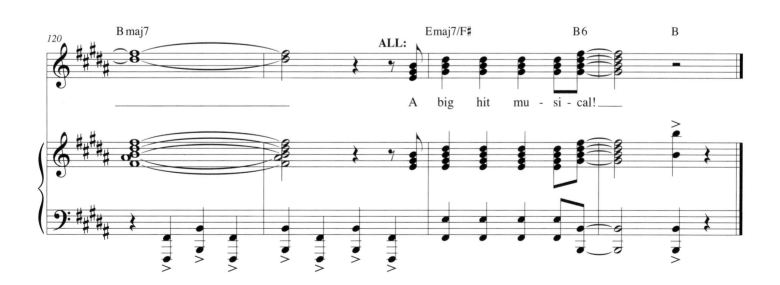

THE BLACK DEATH

Words and Music by
WAYNE KIRKPATRICK
and KAREY KIRKPATRICK

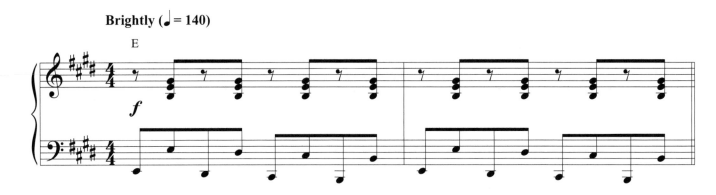

Copyright © 2015 Mad Mother Music and Really Rotten Music
All Rights for Mad Mother Music Administered by Razor & Tie Music Publishing, LLC
All Rights for Really Rotten Music Administered by WB Music Corp.
All Rights Reserved   Used by Permission

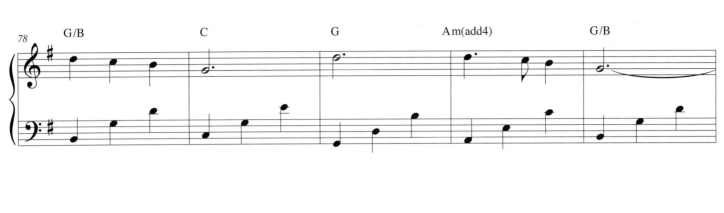
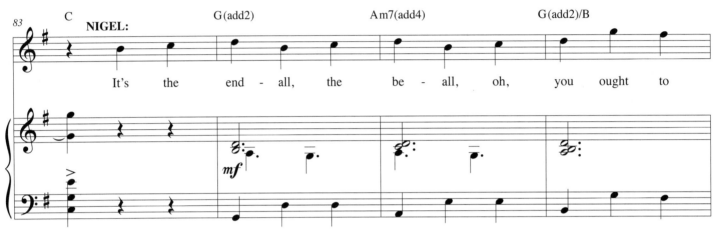
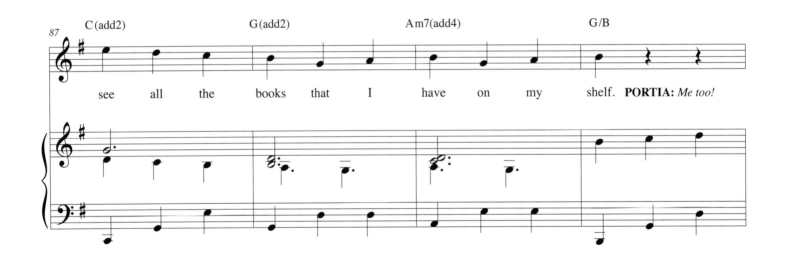
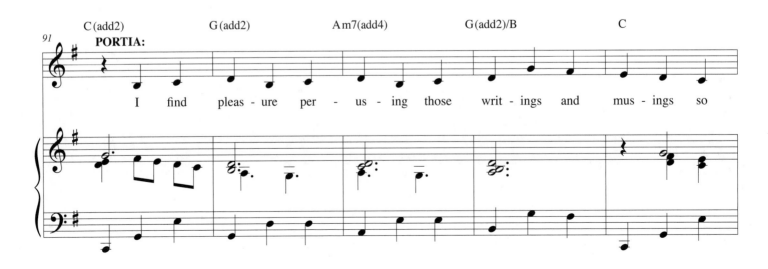

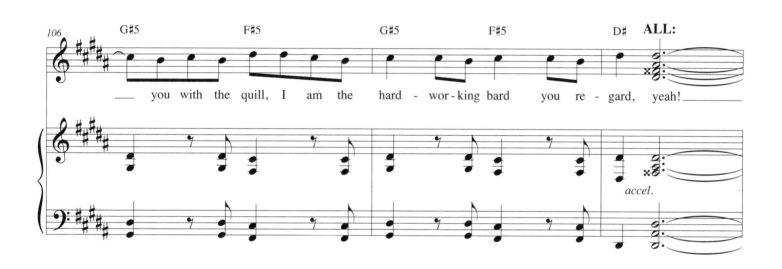
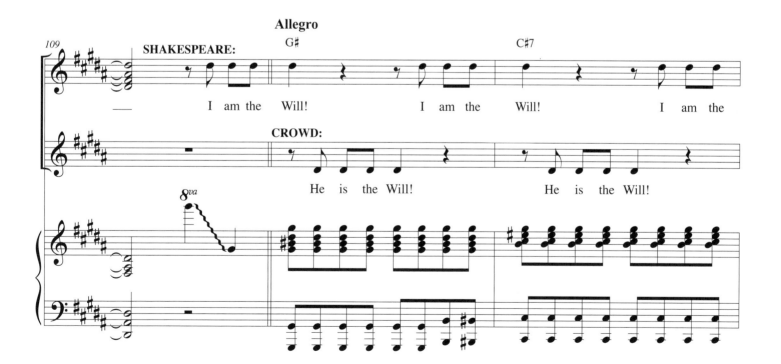

BOTTOM'S GONNA BE ON TOP

Words and Music by
WAYNE KIRKPATRICK
and KAREY KIRKPATRICK

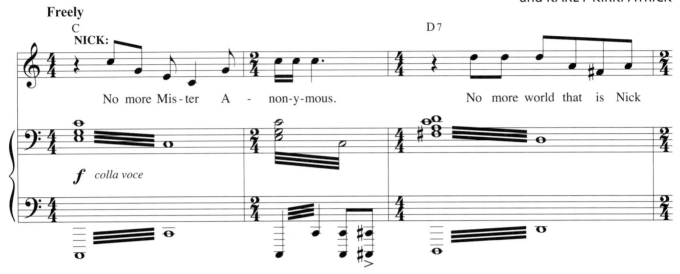

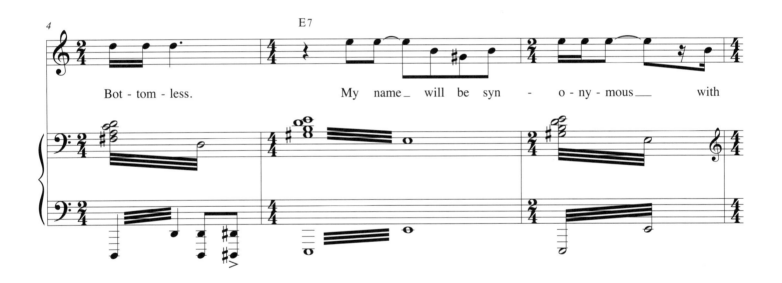

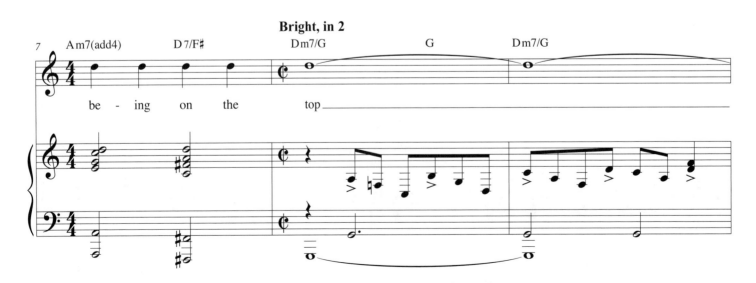

Copyright © 2015 Mad Mother Music and Really Rotten Music
All Rights for Mad Mother Music Administered by Razor & Tie Music Publishing, LLC
All Rights for Really Rotten Music Administered by WB Music Corp.
All Rights Reserved   Used by Permission

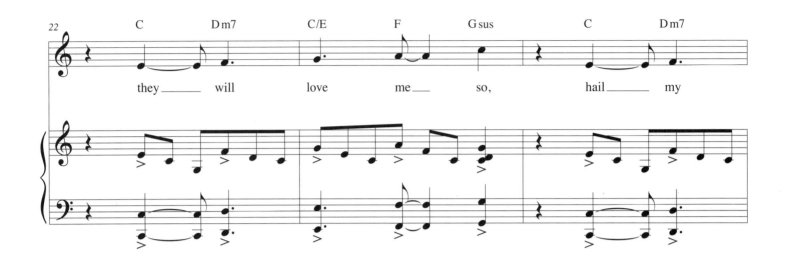
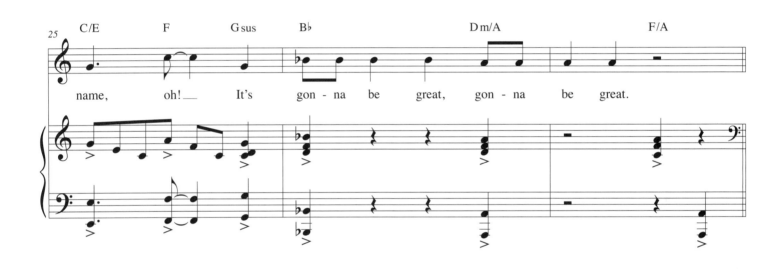

78

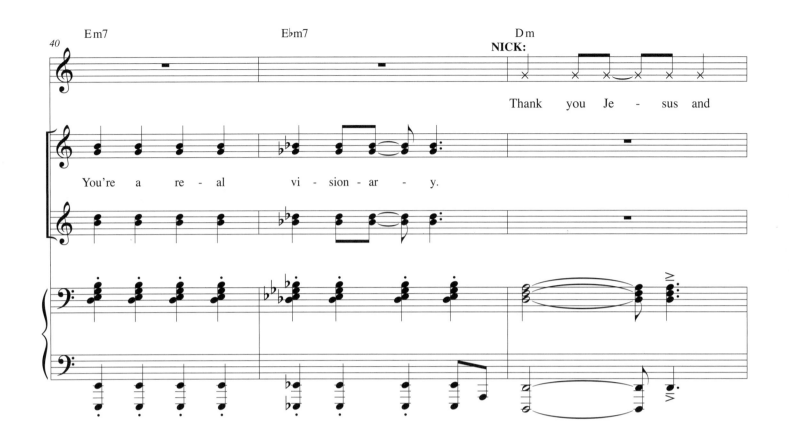

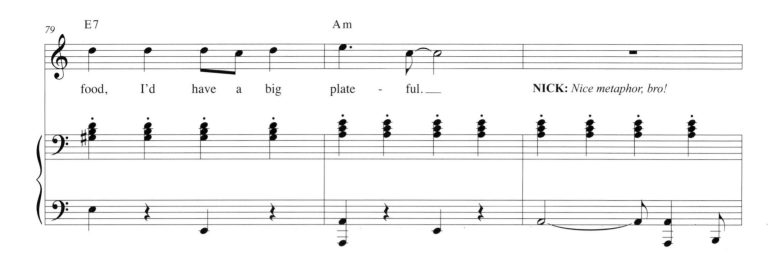
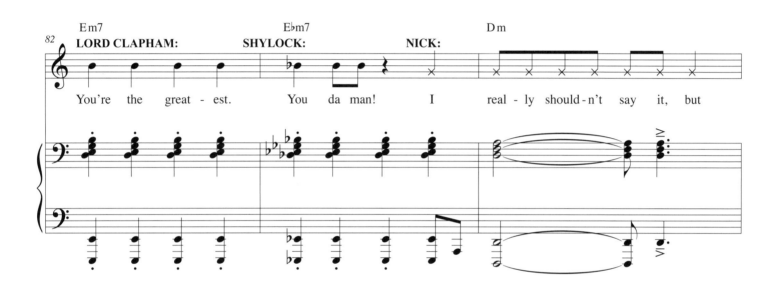
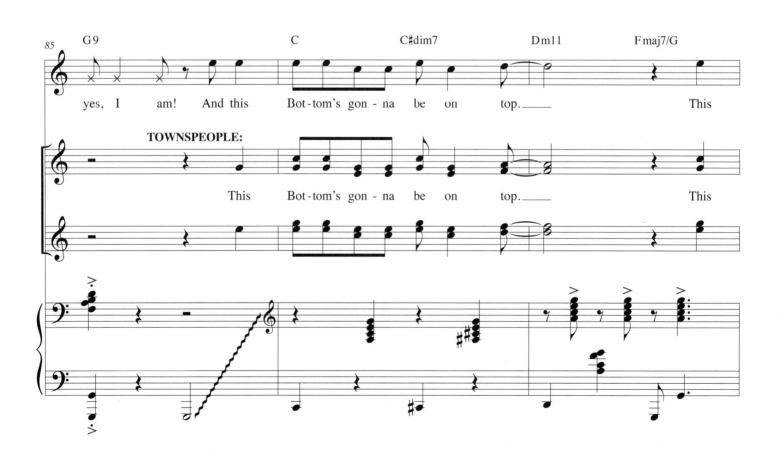

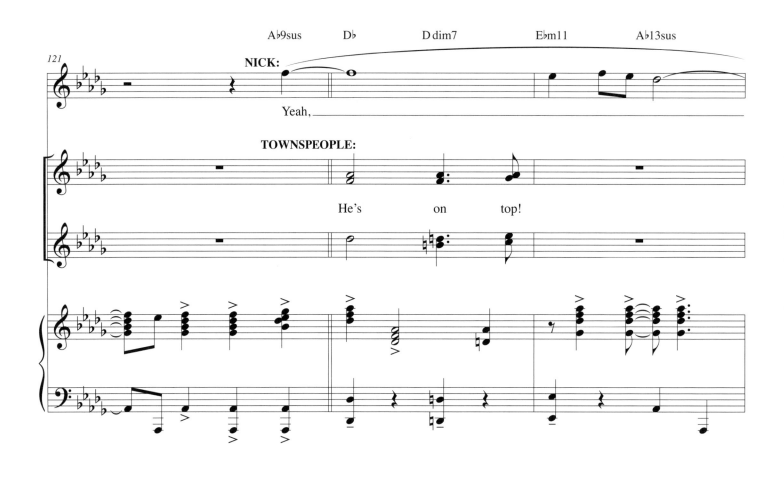
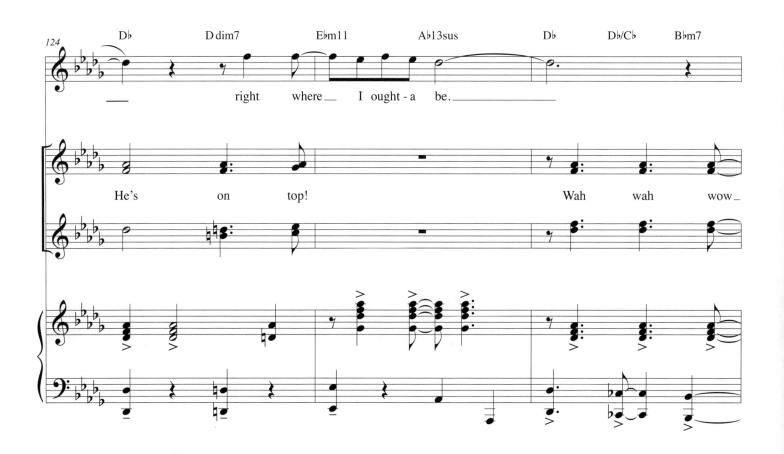

VALET: *Sir...?*
SHAKESPEARE: *Helloooo.....!*
VALET: *You asked for information on what Nicholas Bottom is writing. Our spy is here with news.*
SHAKESPEARE: *Did he see me losing it?*
VALET: *He's half blind, sir.*
SHAKESPEARE: *Oh, good. Then he only saw half of it. Ha ha, see what I did? Speak, man. What news?*

EYEPATCH MAN: *I saw Nick Bottom, I did. He paid a soothsayer to foresee what Shakespeare's greatest play would be.*
SHAKESPEARE: *<GASP> That sneaky little thief! Why doesn't he get his own idea!?*

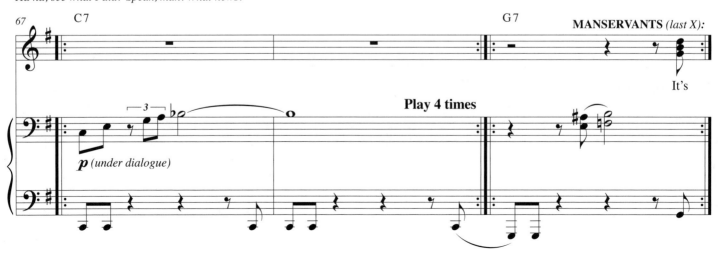

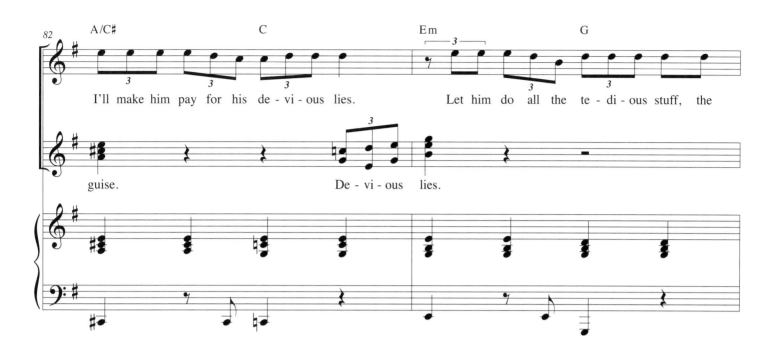
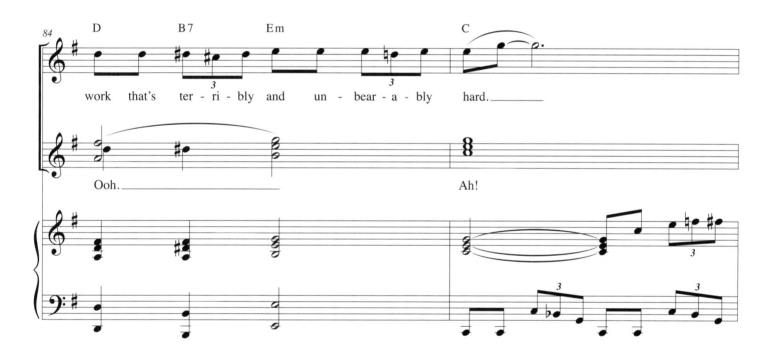

WE SEE THE LIGHT

Words and Music by
WAYNE KIRKPATRICK
and KAREY KIRKPATRICK

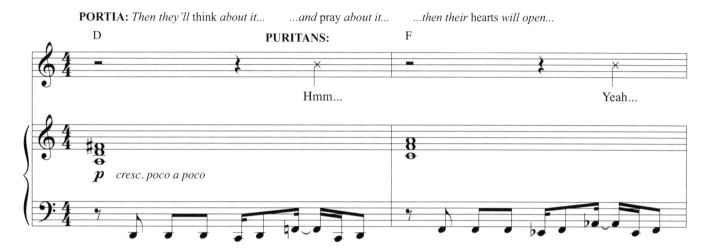

Copyright © 2015 Mad Mother Music and Really Rotten Music
All Rights for Mad Mother Music Administered by Razor & Tie Music Publishing, LLC
All Rights for Really Rotten Music Administered by WB Music Corp.
All Rights Reserved   Used by Permission

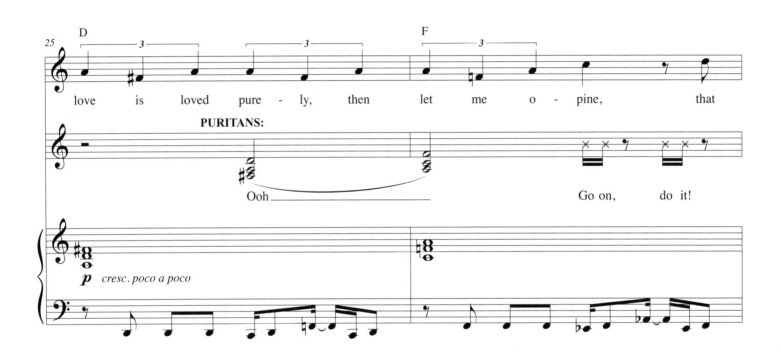

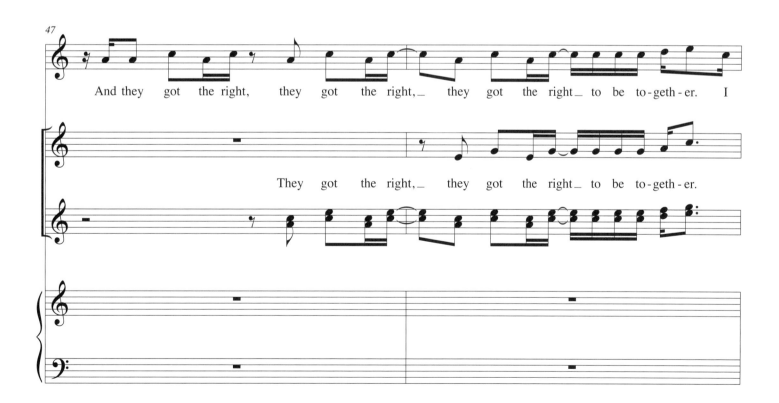

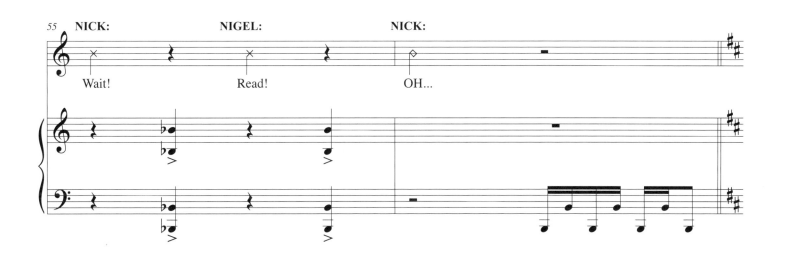

MAKE AN OMELETTE

Words and Music by
WAYNE KIRKPATRICK
and KAREY KIRKPATRICK

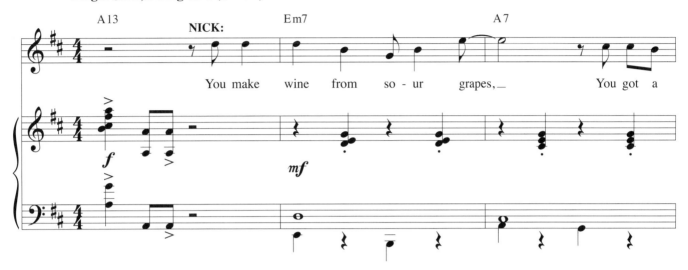
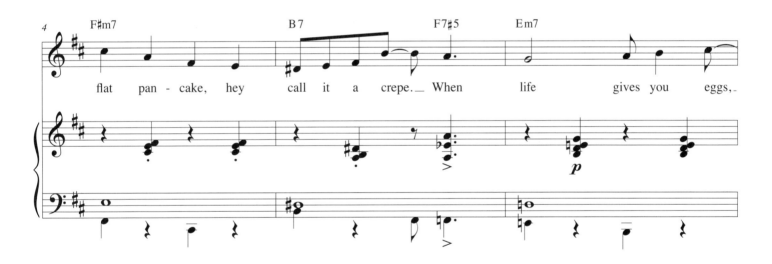

Copyright © 2015 Mad Mother Music and Really Rotten Music
All Rights for Mad Mother Music Administered by Razor & Tie Music Publishing, LLC
All Rights for Really Rotten Music Administered by WB Music Corp.
All Rights Reserved   Used by Permission

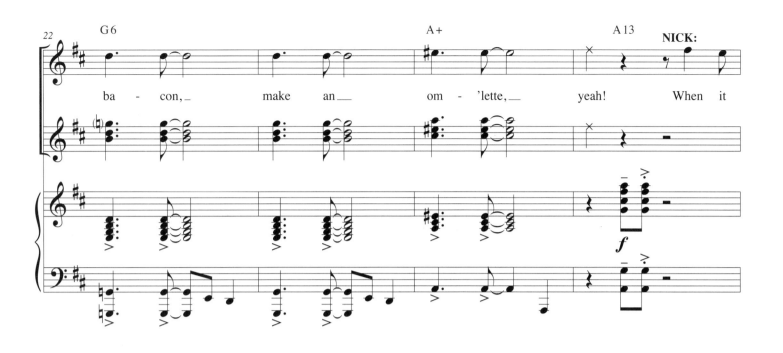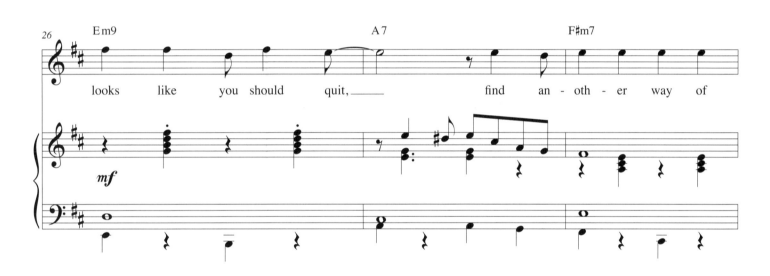

TO THINE OWN SELF BE TRUE
(Reprise)

Words and Music by
WAYNE KIRKPATRICK
and KAREY KIRKPATRICK

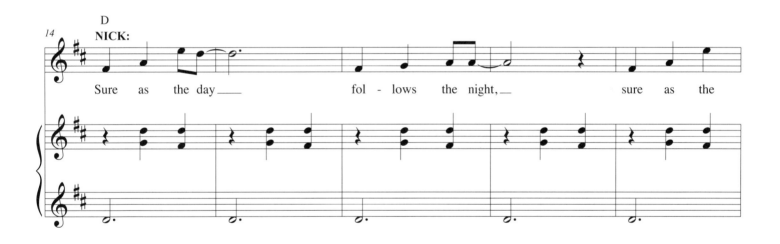

Sure as the day ____ fol-lows the night, ____ sure as the

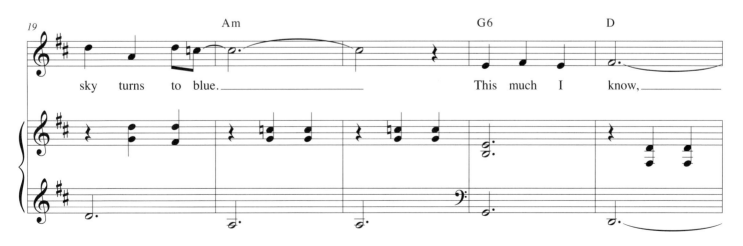

sky turns to blue. _____ This much I know, ____

Copyright © 2015 Mad Mother Music and Really Rotten Music
All Rights for Mad Mother Music Administered by Razor & Tie Music Publishing, LLC
All Rights for Really Rotten Music Administered by WB Music Corp.
All Rights Reserved   Used by Permission